101 Amazing Things to Do in Barcelona

G000165905

Introduction

So you're going to Barcelona, huh? You are very lucky indeed! You are sure in for a treat because Barcelona is, without a doubt, one of the most special travel destinations on the face of the earth. It offers something for every visitor, so whether you are into exploring the Catalan cuisine, unforgettable adventures on the beach, or celebrating with locals at music festivals, this city has something for you.

In this guide, we'll be giving you the low down on:
- the very best things to shove in your pie hole, whether you want to chow down on the best paella you've ever had or you fancy sipping on a glass of Cava or two
- incredible festivals, from epic summer festivals like Primavera Sound through to the celebrations of the Summer Solstice
- the coolest historical and cultural sights that you simply cannot afford to miss like stunning buildings from Gaudi, and world class art museums
- the most incredible outdoor adventures, whether you want to sail across the coast of the city or you'd like to scale a climbing wall

- where to shop for authentic souvenirs so that you can remember your trip to Barcelona forever
- the places where you can party like a local and make new friends
- and tonnes more coolness besides!

Let's not waste any more time – here are the 101 most amazing, spectacular, and cool things not to miss in Barcelona!

1. Stroll Around the Botanical Gardens of Barcelona

Thanks to the wide, open streets of Barcelona, this is a city that feels very spacious, and not too crowded. But if you are somebody who needs lots of green and might feel overwhelmed by city life, somewhere you can escape to for a morning is the Botanical Gardens of Barcelona. The gardens specialise in plants from Mediterranean climates, with various sections such as Australia, Chile, California, and South Africa.

(Carrer del Doctor Font i Quer, 2, 08038 Barcelona; http://museuciencies.cat/visitans/jardi-botanic)

2. Eat Seafood With Locals at La Cova Fumada

One of the greatest pleasures of visiting a city by the coast is that you get to chow down on lots and lots of fresh seafood. Of course, you'll find plenty of seafood restaurants in Barcelona, but our pick of the bunch is called La Cova Fumada, located in the port area of the city. The food here is rustic and the atmosphere is relaxed – and you'll be eating alongside locals while tucking into things like razor clams with garlic, and fresh crawfish.

(Carrer del Baluart, 56, 08003 Barcelona)

3. Party Hard at Primavera Sound

Barcelona is one of the very best destinations in Europe for summer partying and summer festivals, and one festival that indie and alternative fans won't want to miss is called Primavera Sound, and it takes place at the end of May or beginning of June each year. This festival is more and more successful each year because of its incredible line-up. Acts that have taken to the stage in previous years include The XX, Arcade Fire, and Grace Jones.
(www.primaverasound.es/?lang=en)

4. Discover Diverse Artworks at European Museum of Modern Art

One of the most underrated art museums in Barcelona would have to be the European Museum of Modern Art, which is dedicated to showcasing a vast selection of contemporary and modern art, but all of it is figurative, so don't worry if you are baffled by abstract art pieces – there's none of that here. A huge focus is placed on temporary exhibits, so you can see something new and exciting every time that you visit.
(Carrer de la Barra de Ferro, 5, 08003 Barcelona; www.meam.es)

5. Take in the Light Show of the Magic Fountain of Montjuic

To enjoy Barcelona, it's not necessary to spend lots of money on expensive tickets for shows or to empty your wallet at fancy cocktail bars because there are just as many free attractions. And something that never fails to make us feel all warm and fuzzy inside is the incredible light show of the Fountain of Montjuic. It was created in 1929 for the International Exhibition, and it has a display of music, water acrobatics, and lights of more than 50 colours. *(http://lameva.barcelona.cat/es/aprovechala/fuente-magica)*

6. Be Wowed by Gaudi's Iconic Sagrada Familia

There are some buildings around the world that just everybody knows and can identify because they are that iconic. Gaudi's famous Sagrada Familia in Barcelona is most certainly one of those buildings. This Roman Catholic cathedral has been a work in progress for practically all of its existence, and at the time of Gaudi's death it was actually only about 25% complete. There's currently some building work happening on the site, but it's still a must visit while in Barcelona.

(Carrer de Mallorca, 401, 08013 Barcelona; www.sagradafamilia.org/index.html)

7. Get on Board With Local Art at the Museu Nacional d'Art de Catalunya

If you're an artsy kind of person, you are definitely in the right city because Barcelona is one of the underrated arts gems of Europe in our opinion. One of the museums you shouldn't miss, particularly if you want to get to grips with the local arts culture, is the National Museum of Catalan Art. The Museum is housed inside the gorgeous National Palace, and takes you on a journey of 1000 years of Catalan art. Highlights include Romanesque church paintings and the modern art collections with works from the 19th and 20th centuries.

(Palau Nacional, Parc de Montjuïc, s/n, 08038 Barcelona; www.museunacional.cat/en)

8. Shop for Treasures at Barcelona Vintage Market

While you are in Spain, there's no doubt that you will want to take back some treasures that will always remind you of your trip. Our advice would be to avoid the shops that are specifically targeted towards tourists, and head to some of the local markets instead – and there are plenty of them! Our top tip for Barcelona is the Barcelona Vintage Market. You'll find everything from vintage furniture to antique jewellery and vinyl records. So get shopping. *(www.barcelonavintagemarket.com)*

9. Have a Lusty Afternoon in Barcelona's Erotic Museum

Barcelona has many standout attractions, which make it the go-to destination of Europe, but we have been to Barcelona so many times that we really like to get off the beaten track and check out some of the attractions that are more hidden away. Take the Erotic Museum, for example, which is ideal when you're in a bit of a lusty mood. It contains 800 objects that relate to eroticism right from Ancient Rome and Greece and up to the present day. *(La Rambla, 96 bis, 08002 Barcelona; www.erotica-museum.com)*

10. Have an Exquisite Evening at Barcelona's Tandem Cocktail Bar

Let's face it, you aren't going to have too much trouble finding a wonderful place to have a drink or two in Barcelona, but actually, there is so much choice that it can be overwhelming. When we are pondering where to go for a cocktail, Tandem Cocktail Bar is always a safe bet. This is an old school place with bartenders dressed up in white shirts and black jackets. But it's not all for show – the drinks are just as snazzy, and we are particularly fond of their Gin Fizz.

(Carrer d'Aribau, 86, 08036 Barcelona; www.tandemcocktail.com)

11. Party in the Street at Barcelona's La Merce Festival

Barcelona is a fantastic party city at absolutely any time of the year, but it's at the end of September that Barcelona feels particularly festive for the annual La Merce Festival, which takes place on September 24th every year. The festival is a celebration of Barcelona's Patron Saint, Virgin de la Merce, with many fun events including a procession of giant wooden figures through the city.

12. Ogle the Surrealist Sculptures at Parc de Joan Miro

Barcelona is one of those cities that just has it all. As well as incredible shopping streets, wonderful eateries, and beaches, there's also an abundance of green spaces, and one of the most unique green spaces that you will find in Barcelona is the Parc de Joan Miro, which unsurprisingly is a park that contains sculptures created by Miro. There's also plenty of green space, so why not pack a picnic, and enjoy a leisurely day in the Spanish sunshine?

(Carrer d'Aragó, 2, 08015 Barcelona;
http://lameva.barcelona.cat/es/aprovechala/parques-y-
jardines/parque-de-joan-miro_92086012013.html)

13. Get to Grips With Barcelona's History at Museu d'Historia de Barcelona

Barcelona is a city that has it all. If you want to walk the streets and look at the architecture, or if you want to eat lots of pinchos and drink sangria, you can do it. And if you want more of a cultural trip, there's also a fantastic museum scene, and we'd advise going to the Museu d'Historia de Barcelona which tells the story of Barcelona from Roman times and up to the present day. One of the obscure highlights we love is the remains of a Roman salt fish and garum factory.

(Plaça del Rei, s/n, 08002 Barcelona; http://museuhistoria.bcn.cat)

14. Chow Down on Bombas While in Barcelona

Bomba is an interesting word in Barcelona. It literally means "bomb", it can also be used as a slang word that means something along the lines of "cool", and it is also a local type of food in Barcelona that we just can't get enough of. These little bombs are essentially a mix of meat and potatoes that are deep fried and slathered in tomato sauce. They are filling and a slightly different taste of Spain that you will only find in Barcelona.

15. Take in a Concert at a Stunning Barcelona Concert Hall

Barcelona is a great place for budget travellers because simply walking the streets and taking in the incredible architecture is a wonderful attraction in itself. One of our favourite buildings is a 19th century concert hall called the

Palau de la Musica Catalana, and it has been constructed in a Catalan Modernist style with swirls and dynamic forms taking precedence over straight lines. And if you did have a little money left in your budget, do take in a live concert there for an unforgettable experience.

(C/ Palau de la Música, 4-6, 08003 Barcelona; www.palaumusica.cat)

16. Tuck Into Traditional Barcelona Tapas at Euskal Etxea

Barcelona is a delightful city for filling your stomach, and no trip to Barcelona would be complete without filling up on pintxos, which are essentially small plates, or tapas. And our favourite places for pintxos while we're in the city is a local haunt called Euskal Etxea. Almost everything consists of something atop a slice of crusty bread, whether it's a slice of cheese, a type of ham, or some kind of seafood. It's simple, yes, but it totally works. Their ciders are also worth a try.

(Placeta de Montcada, 1, 08003 Barcelona; http://gruposagardi.com/restaurante/euskal-etxea-taberna)

17. Party in the Open Air at Barcelona's La Terrrazza

The Barcelona sunshine is one of our favourite things in the entire world. It's a place where it's typically sunny throughout the year, and even in the winter time it's not particularly cold. And our favourite way of enjoying the sunshine of Barcelona is by partying in the open air at La Terrrazza. Head there in the early evening if you want a quiet cocktail, or arrive after midnight if you want to party hard into the night in the balmy open air of Catalonia. *(Avenida Francesc Ferrer I Guardia, 0 S N (Poble Espanyol), 08001 Barcelona; http://laterrrazza.com)*

18. Walk Through the Sewers of Barcelona

As you walk along the wide, tree lined streets of Barcelona, you will only see a very polished city with a reputation for being one of the most liveable places on the planet. But there is an underside to this city that you won't see as you walk around. Believe it or not, the 19th century sewers, the foundations of which were laid in the Medieval period, are open to the public for exploration. As you are guided around, you'll get to know the history of the tunnels, of sanitation in Barcelona, and of folklore relating to the sewers.

19. Wave a Rainbow Flag for Barcelona Pride

If you are an LGBT traveller, you'll be pleased to know that Spain is one of the most gay friendly countries on the face of the earth, with a vibrant gay culture in virtually every city across the country. Barcelona is no different, and if you really want to experience the city when it comes to life with gay exuberance, be sure to make it to the annual Gay Pride event, which takes place at the end of June each year. There's a huge range of fun parties and events, and the whole thing culminates in an epic street parade through the centre of the city.

(www.pridebarcelona.org/en)

20. Learn to Speak Some Catalan

If you are planning to stick around in Barcelona for an extended period of time, it can be a great idea to get to grips with the local language so that you can better communicate with the local people. But what language is that exactly? Yes, everyone in Barcelona speaks Spanish, but if you really want to win over the locals, taking the time to learn some Catalan would be a better choice. The EOI Language School has a very good reputation. *(www.eoibd.cat/en)*

21. Indulge a Sweet Tooth With Crema Catalana

Crema Catalana is one of those incredible, decadent desserts that seems to please every palette, and that even the lactose intolerant have a hard time resisting. This is, essentially, the local Catalan take on a French dessert you are no doubt familiar with: crème brulee. The difference with this version is that the custard is flavoured with orange peel and cinnamon, which, in our opinion, makes it even more delicious than its French counterpart.

22. Look at Iconic Artworks at the Museu Picasso

Picasso is, of course, one of the most iconic painters in the history of art, and a source of national pride for Spain. While he was born in the south of Spain, in Malaga, it's in Barcelona that you can find one of the largest museums dedicated solely to this masters' artworks, the Museu Picasso. In fact, there's over 4000 Picasso works in the permanent collection alone, so it's more than possible to spend a few days walking around the building and checking out the masterpieces.

(Carrer Montcada, 15-23, 08003 Barcelona; www.museupicasso.bcn.cat)

23. Take in a View of the City From Bunkers Del Carmel

If you fancy getting a little bit off the beaten path while you're in Barcelona, be sure to check out some of the lesser visited neighbourhoods such as charming El Carmel. Once there, head up the hill where you will find a viewpoint called Bunkers del Carmel. The platforms are actually disused firing platforms from the Spanish civil war, but now they simply offer an incredible 360 degree panorama of all the city.

(Carrer de Marià Lavèrnia, s/n, 08032 Barcelona)

24. Learn Something New at the Maritime Museum of Barcelona

One of the lesser known gems of Barcelona's museum scene is the Maritime Museum, which is great for a couple of hours on a cloudy morning, or simply if you want to learn something new. Spain, does of course, have an incredible naval history (hello Christopher Columbus!) and this museum really represents that breadth of history. There are many interactive exhibits that make this a fun place to take kids, but the highlight is a life size replica of Santa Maria, the ship on which Columbus sailed in 1492. *(Av. de les Drassanes, s/n, 08001 Barcelona; www.mmb.cat)*

25. Catch an Opera at the Teatre del Liceu

If you have packed your finest clothes to Barcelona, and you are looking for an opportunity to get all dressed up, we can think of no better evening out than at the iconic Teatre del Liceu. This theatre is located on the famous pedestrian street, Las Ramblas, and opened way back in 1847. This is the place to catch a grand ballet or opera performance, with world class performers and stunning acoustics. The theatre can host more than 2000 guests across six levels.

(La Rambla, 51-59, 08002 Barcelona; www.liceubarcelona.cat)

26. Get Geeky at CosmoCaixa Barcelona

Barcelona is very much an artsy and cultural city, but if you are more taken by science than the arts, you don't have to miss out on the fun, at least not if you include a trip to CosmoCaixa Barcelona in your travel itinerary. Some highlights include the Flooded Forest, a place where visitors can enjoy the wet and dry environs of the Amazon rainforest, and the Hall of Matter, which will take you on a journey of evolution from the Big Bang.

(Carrer d' Isaac Newton, 26, 08022 Barcelona; www.cosmocaixa.com)

27. Try Windsurfing at Base Nautica

If you love adventure activities, Barcelona would probably not be the first travel destination that springs to mind, but actually you can enjoy things like surfing kitesurfing and windsurfing there. If you've not tried windsurfing before, it's basically a mixture of surfing and sailing, and your board will have a sail on it to propel you through the ocean. There is a popular place called Base Nautica where you can rent all the equipment you need and take lessons.

(Av. del Litoral, s/n, 08005 Barcelona; http://basenautica.org)

28. Take in the Majesty of the National Palace of Montjuic

Without a shadow of a doubt, one of the most iconic buildings that you will find anywhere in Barcelona is the National Palace of Montjuic, which you can find on the Montjuic hillside. It was built for the International Expo in 1929, and became the site of the National Art Museum of Catalonia in 1934. You are welcome to enter the grand Oval Hall of the palace free of charge, and take in all of its grandeur.

(Av. dels Montanyans, S/N, 08038 Barcelona; www.museunacional.cat)

29. Indulge a Chocolate Fiend at Museu de la Xocolata

There are two types of people in this life: people who would do anything for a morsel of sweet chocolate, and people who we can't begin to understand. If you are a chocolate lover through and through, then make sure that the Museum de la Xocolata is part of your Barcelona itinerary. But this is no ordinary chocolate museum, because it showcases the history of Europe through various chocolate sculptures. You will also learn about the origins of chocolate and its Mayan roots.

(Carrer del Comerç, 36, 08003 Barcelona; www.museuxocolata.cat)

30. Get Close to Sea Life at L'Aquarium

If you are travelling with kids, one of the places you can visit for an afternoon to keep them amused and entertained is L'Aquarium, Barcelona's main aquarium. There are 11,000 animals there representing 450 species of sea life, so there is plenty to see. You'll be able to get up close to sharks, rays, octopus, and many other things. You can even descend into a shark tank inside a cage if you are brave enough!

(Moll d'Espanya del Port Vell, s/n, 08039 Barcelona; www.aquariumbcn.com)

31. Have a Climbing Adventure at Climbat La Foixarda

If you are the kind of person who prefers to get active on holiday to endless beach days, a place that you might want to check out is called Climbat La Foixarda. This is one of the most epic climbing gyms that we have ever been to anywhere in the world. It has a height of over 15 metres and you can even climb over the ceiling.

(Carrer de la Foixarda, 14-18, 08038 Barcelona; www.climbat.com/la-foixarda-barcelona/en)

32. Sample the Cheeses of Catalonia at Formatgeria La Seu

Europe is, of course, one of the best spots for cheese tasting and cheese buying, and as one of the best loved cities of Europe, Barcelona is most certainly a place where cheese lovers can indulge. If you only make it to one cheese shop during your time in the city, make sure that it's Formatgeria La Seu. Located in the Gothic Quarter, on the site of one of the city's first butter factories, this cheesemongers specialises in local Catalan cheeses, and the friendly staff will help you choose a cheese (or five) that you will love.

(Carrer de la Dagueria, 16, 08002 Barcelona; www.formatgerialaseu.com)

33. Indulge a Sports Buff at the FC Barcelona Museum

If you are a total sport fanatic, you are probably already familiar with Spain's strong commitment to football (soccer), and if you'd like to know more about this national obsession, be sure to pay a trip to the FC Barcelona Museum, located at Camp Nou, the epic stadium where the local football team play home games. This is one of the most popular museums in the whole city, and with good reason. You can see artefacts relating to local players and their careers, and tour the impressive stadium grounds.

(C. d'Aristides Maillol, s/n, 08028 Barcelona; www.fcbarcelona.cat)

34. Learn Something New at the Museum of Catalan History

Ask a local person in Barcelona whether they identify as Spanish or Catalan, and the majority will tell you that they are Catalan, and that's why it can be a very good idea to learn something about the Catalan history and identity. And what better place to do just that than at the Museum of History of Catalonia? You'll get to grips with how the Romans lived in Barcelona, you can learn about the Arab occupation of the city, and even descend into a civil-war air raid shelter.

(Palau de Mar, Plaça de Pau Vila, 3, 08003 Barcelona; www.mhcat.cat)

35. Celebrate a World of Gastronomy at Van Van Market

When in Barcelona, it's imperative that you put as much food in your mouth as humanly possible. That can be a tricky and expensive exercise if you have to wander from restaurant to restaurant, but the monthly Van Van Market makes it easy. This gastronomic market is exclusively for food trucks, so you can purchase gourmet burgers from one truck, churros from another, and a few beers from yet another – perfect.

(www.vanvanmarket.com)

36. Enjoy Some Volleyball on Mar Bella Beach

When the Olympics came to Barcelona in 1992, the city underwent a huge amount of redevelopment, and this means that some beaches were created that were never even there before! One of these is Mar Bella Beach, and it's still enduringly popular, particularly with people who love fun beach activities. There are volleyball nets erected on the beach so you can challenge your beach neighbours to match, and there's also table tennis, sailing, and other activities to enjoy.

37. Visit a Museum Dedicated to Cannabis

The Hemp Museum Gallery is certainly one of the strangest museums to be found in Barcelona, but if you are interested in cannabis culture and have a spare hour or two, it could make for a great way to pass some time. And actually, the collection here is pretty impressive. You can find over 8000 objects related to cannabis, and you can learn everything from the production of the plant to its manufacture, from its use in ancient rituals through to its benefits in modern medicine.

(Carrer Ample, 35, 08002 Barcelona; http://hashmuseum.com)

38. Visit Gaudi's Wonky Wavy House, Casa Mila

Gaudi is, of course, an architect and visionary who is synonymous with the city of Barcelona, and we'd happily spend our Barcelona trip walking the streets and taking in the strange majesty of his constructions. One of his buildings that you really mustn't miss is called Casa Mila, and has a wavy exterior. It was built between the years 1906 and 1912, and now contains a cultural centre and has been recognised with UNESCO World Heritage status. *(Provença, 261-265, 08008 Barcelona; www.lapedrera.com/ca/home)*

39. Entertain the Kids at Tibidabo Amusement Park

Travelling with kids can be extremely rewarding but it's also hard work. You want to give them memories that last for years, but it's a challenge to keep kids occupied at all times. If they don't want to go to another museum, give them a break and head to the Tibidabo Amusement Park. This is one of the oldest amusement parks on the whole continent, and retains and old-world charm. Be sure to take a ride on the Big Wheel for magnificent views across the city.

(Plaça Tibidabo, 3-4, 08035 Barcelona; www.tibidabo.cat)

40. Soak up Some Rays on Barceloneta Beach

Barcelona is truly the city that has it all. You can fill your days with incredible cultural experiences, you can party on all night with the locals, and if you want to spend endless lazy days on the beach, you have that option too. There's a number of really lovely beaches in Barcelona, and one of our favourites goes by the name of Barceloneta. You might think of this as the main beach in the city, and it's a lovely, fun social space, so it might not be the best place if you want peace and quiet.

41. Take in Some Outdoor Cinema at Montjuic Castle Gardens

If you love cinema, then you should make sure to plan your trip to Barcelona to coincide with the Sala Montjuic Open Air Film Festival. This is no ordinary film festival because all of the screenings take place in the gorgeous gardens of Montjuic Castle. There is bound to be something that you love in the programme of films because the festival is known for screening classic movies like Manhattan and Spotlight. It's hosted across July each year.

(http://salamontjuic.org/en)

42. Cool Yourself Down With a Granizado

If you visit Spain during the summertime, you'll definitely be looking for some ways to cool down. Take a look around you and you'll see that one of the most popular ways for locals to cope with the heat is by slurping on a granizado. A granizado is essentially the Spanish version of a slushy, and it can come in a variety of delicious flavours. If you are wondering where to grab one for yourself, head to one of the many ice cream parlours around.

43. Eat all the Deliciousness at the La Boqueria Market

One of our favourite things to do in a new city is walk the aisles of an incredible market, and they are not much more incredible than La Boqueria in Barcelona, which has a long and illustrious history in the city that dates all the way back to the 13th century. This is the best place to discover all the best ingredients of Catalonia, with an abundance of colourful fruits and veggies, seafood, and also a smattering of tapas bars where you can sit and have a nibble and a glass of wine.

(La Rambla, 91, 08001 Barcelona; www.boqueria.info)

44. Take in all the Glory of Santa Maria del Mar Church

Architecture buffs will have one hell of a time in Barcelona. Of course, there are the famous buildings designed by Gaudi, but this city is also filled with incredible religious architecture. One of the most impressive churches in the city is the Santa Maria del Mar church. This building took more than 50 years to build in the 14th century, and is an incredible example of the Catalan Gothic style. The interior is beautifully light and spacious, and a perfect place to escape the city's heat and enjoy some serenity.

(Plaça de Santa Maria, 1, 08003 Barcelona; www.santamariadelmarbarcelona.org)

45. Take in a Concert at the Palau de la Musica Catalana

If you want to have a glamorous night out while in Barcelona, there's quite a few options, but we think that a night at the Palau de la Music Catalana is something totally unforgettable. This concert hall was constructed at the beginning of the 20th century, and you can catch all kinds of music performances there, so whether you want to listen to a symphony, hear a contemporary jazz performance, or you want to get to grips with local Catalan music, the choice is yours.

(C/ Palau de la Música, 4-6, 08003 Barcelona; www.palaumusica.cat)

46. Taste Barcelona's Best Cava at La Vinya del Senyor

Want to head outside for a quiet glass of wine with a loved one? Then we would totally recommend booking a table at La Vinya del Senyor. This is a place that true wine buffs will appreciate because the wines they offer are very carefully selected, and the staff are extremely knowledgeable about everything that's in stock. We are especially impressed by their collection of local Cavas. There's only a few tables so be sure to book ahead.

(Plaza Sta Maria, 5, 08003 Barcelona)

47. Go Shoe Shopping at La Manual Alpargatera

A fine pair of beautiful shoes is one of the simple pleasures that life has to offer, and if you love shoes you should head to a studio called La Manual Alpargatera, which only sells shoes and shoe related things. It opened all the way back in 1943, and specialised in homemade espadrilles, the style of which wasn't very popular at the time. These days, people flock internationally for these handmade shoes, and with prices starting at just 10 Euros, it's possible to find a stylish bargain.

(Carrer d'Avinyó, 7, 08002 Barcelona; www.lamanualalpargatera.es)

48. Visit Casa Batllo, One of Barcelona's Most Iconic Buildings

Casa Batllo is one of the places that you will find in all of the guidebooks, but it really is such an iconic and beautiful building that we had to include it on this list of places you have to check out in Barcelona. The whole of the façade is decorated with colourful ceramic tiles and the roof has been likened to the hunched back of a dragon. The inside is just as bonkers as the outside so do take your time walking around.

(Passeig de Gràcia, 43, 08007 Barcelona; www.casabatllo.es)

49. Take in the Dynamic Sculpture of Frank Gehry's Fish

Barcelona is a city that is crammed filled with all kinds of details and treasures that arts lovers will adore. Frank Gehry is, of course, one of the most influential and famous architects in the world, and you can see one of his works in Barcelona as well. This is not a building but a stainless steel sculpture created to resemble a fish and called El Peix. It was created for the 1992 Olympics and sits on the seafront.

(Carrer de Ramon Trias Fargas 1. 08005 Barcelona)

50. Eat Lots of Tasty Things at Mercat de Santa Caterina

There's no doubt that one of the best ways to experience a city is to eat lots of delicious local treats, and this is particularly true in a city like Barcelona that truly has a gastronomic scene that is second to none. The actual structure of the market is stunning, with a wavy multi-coloured roof, but it's what's inside that really pleases us. The produce here is all fresh, so whether you want to stock up on some local fruits or delicious ham, the choice is yours.

(Av. de Francesc Cambó, 16, 08003 Barcelona)

51. Get Cultural at the CCCB

If you are a culture vulture at heart, you need to know about the CCCB, which stands for Centre de Cultura Contemporania de Barcelona, or the Contemporary Culture Centre of Barcelona. No matter what type of cultural experiences you are into, you are sure to find something stimulating there. Whether you would like to attend a contemporary art exhibition, take in some performance art, or watch an avant-garde film screening, it's all there for the taking.

(Carrer de Montalegre, 5, 08001 Barcelona; www.cccb.org/en)

52. Party the Night Away at Salt Beach Club

One thing that local people in Barcelona sure are good at is partying the night away, and if you are a party monster you have a whole lot of bars and nightclubs to choose from. One of the best of the bunch is Salt Beach Club. We love it because, as the name suggests, this place is slap bang in the middle of the beach, and it's managed by the W Hotel, so it's totally stylish and cool. See you there for a cocktail.

(Passeig del Mare Nostrum, 19-21, 08039 Barcelona; www.saltbeachclub.com)

53. Enjoy all the Action of Festival Grec de Barcelona

The Montjuic hills are home to an open air performance space called Teatre Grec. It's great to watch a show there at any time, but it really comes to life during July, when it hosts the annual Festival Grec de Barcelona throughout the whole month. This arts festival has something for everyone with drama, dance, music, and even circus performances. The festival has attracted talent such as Peter Brook, Dario Fo, and Bob Dylan.

(http://lameva.barcelona.cat/grec/en)

54. Take in the Sculptures at Museu Frederic Mares

Frederic Mares might not be such a famous name as an artist like Picasso, but he is very important to the people of Barcelona, and you can learn more about this local sculptor and obsessive collector at the museum that bears his name. This collection contains many of the incredible items that the man collected (and some that he made) on his travels, some of which date back to the 12th century. The museum also has a delightful courtyard.

(Plaça Sant Iu, 5, 08002 Barcelona; www.museumares.bcn.cat)

55. Find a Bargain at Encants Vells

Want to have some fun shopping experiences while you're in Barcelona? Then forget the high street shopping and head to one of the most popular flea markets in Barcelona, which goes by the name of Encants Vells. Not only is this a great place to find some treasures at rock bottom prices, but it's a historic attraction in its own right, since this market dates all the way back to the 14th century, making it one of the oldest flea markets anywhere in Europe. It's open on Mondays, Wednesdays, Fridays, and Saturdays.

(Carrer de los Castillejos, 158, 08013 Barcelona; www.encantsbcn.com)

56. Tuck Into Artisanal Candies at Papabubble

If you have any kind of sweet tooth at all, then be sure to visit Papabubble while in Barcelona. This sweetshop now has branches all over the world, but it all started in the Catalan capital. They are still committed to using the best flavours to create hand crafted candies, which make for great late night munchies or gifts for friends and families. Kids love to visit because you can actually watch the staff make sweets from scratch.

(Carrer Ample, 28, 08002 Barcelona; www.papabubble.com)

57. Go Rowing in the Parc de la Ciutadella

Barcelona is a very exciting city with plenty to see and do, but when you want some peace, quiet, and tranquillity, be sure to visit the Parc de la Ciutadella. You can simply stroll around and have a picnic on the grass, but if you feel like being a little more active, it can be nice to hire one of the rowing boats on the lake, have a calm rowing experience, and feel that Barcelona sunshine on your face.

(Passeig de Picasso, 21, 08003 Barcelona)

58. Fill Your Stomach at Mercat del Ninot

Mercat del Ninot's translates as The Doll's Market, which really makes no sense because this is a food market through and through, and is a place where you can easily spend a few hours if you are a keen foodie. This is the place to buy fresh produce, whether it's freshly caught seafood or plump and colourful vegetables. If cooking while in Barcelona isn't on your agenda, there are also tapas bars dotted around the market.

(Carrer de Mallorca, 133, 08036 Barcelona; www.mercatdelninot.com)

59. Enjoy the Greenery of Jardins de Joan Maragall

Barcelona is a truly a city that has it all, and even something for people who prefer a slower and more relaxed pace of life. The Jardins de Joan Maragall are spectacular gardens in the city, that are really not on the tourist trail at all (perhaps because they are only open to the public on the weekend). You can expect ornate fountains, ornamental sculptures, and the most perfectly manicured lawns.

(Av. dels Montanyans, 48, 08038 Barcelona)

60. Tuck Into Tasty Catalan Salad, Esqueixada

Those soaring Barcelona temperatures can be really quite hard to deal with sometimes, and it probably means that you'll want to eat light bites instead of heavy meals. One of the lighter dishes in Barcelona, which also happens to be one of the tastiest, is a local salad called Esqueixada. As with most Spanish dishes, it features simple but flavourful ingredients. This salad has shredded salt cod, tomatoes, onions, olive oil, vinegar salt, and sometimes hard boiled eggs.

61. Have a Biking Adventure in Parc de Collserola

Barcelona is a city that is blessed with great weather throughout the year, so it's the perfect travel destination for people who like to spend plenty of their time outdoors in the sunshine. The largest green space in the city is called Parc de Collserola, and it takes up around 80 kilometres of space north of the city centre. If you want to take it easy, pack a picnic and have a stroll around, or if you feel like something more adventurous, there are well marked bike paths through the forest.

(Ctra. de l'Església, 92, 08017 Barcelona; www.parcnaturalcollserola.cat)

62. Discover Some Surrealist Art at Fundacio Joan Miro

There are many famous artists from around Spain, but perhaps the most famous from the city of Barcelona itself is Joan Miro, the surrealist painter and ceramicist who create an incredible output of artwork during the 20th century. The very best place to understand the man and appreciate his works is at Fundacio Joan Miro. The foundation was created by the man himself in the 1970s, and supports the work of other contemporary artists today.

(Parc de Montjuïc, s/n, 08038 Barcelona; www.fmirobcn.org/en)

63. Watch a Flamenco Performance at Tablao de Carmen

Flamenco dancing is a type of Spanish dance that you are probably already faintly familiar with, because of its flair and dramatic red dresses. Although flamenco actually originates from the southern region of Andalucia in Spain, you can catch a fantastic flamenco performance at Tablao de Carmen, a venue that has been putting on its own dramatic flamenco shows for 25 years. Some of Spain's most celebrated flamenco dancers have performed here.

(Av. de Francesc Ferrer i Guàrdia, 13, 08038 Barcelona; www.tablaodecarmen.com)

64. Sail Along the Coastline of the City

If you love nothing more than to feel the sunshine on your face and the breeze in your hair, you should look further afield than Barcelona centre, and perhaps even take to the waters on a boat. Fortunately, there are many companies that can give you a sailing experience along the coast of the city, whether you want to take a trip for a couple of hours, or you'd like to visit somewhere further afield with an overnight stay on a yacht.

65. Get Into the Festival Spirit at Sonar

Sonar is one of the most famous summer music festivals anywhere in the world, and it all originated in Barcelona in 1994. The festival is bigger and better than ever, taking place each year in mid June, and attracting more than 120,000 visitors from over 100 countries all over the world. The festival is committed to booking great talent, as well as an incredible audiovisual show each year. Previous performers have included DJ Shadow and Soulwax. This is a festival for electronic music fans through and through. *(https://sonar.es/en)*

66. Eat an Afternoon Snack of Escalivada

When lunchtime has long gone but you still have a couple of hours until dinner, forget a chocolate bar or bag of crisps, and reach for a local snack instead. We heartily recommend tucking into escalivada, a small plate of delicious grilled vegetables soaked in olive oil. The veggies won't make you so full that you won't be able to eat dinner later, but will give you something tasty to munch on until then.

67. Take Kids Along to the Natural History Museum of Barcelona

The Natural History Museum of Barcelona is a place where your jaw will drop to the floor at the sheer beauty and magnificence of the grandeur of nature, and it's a fantastic place to take kids and have them learn something new. This is also one of the oldest museums in all of the city, since it was founded over 130 years ago. Inside you'll find more than 3 million specimens, with everything from dinosaur fossils to bonsai trees.

(Carrer de Leonardo da Vinci, 4-6, 08019 Barcelona; http://museuciencies.cat)

68. Get Your Caffeine Hit at Onna Café

If you are the kind of person who can't even think about starting the day before having a strong cup of coffee, fear not because you are not alone in this city of coffee aficionados. There's plenty of delightful cafes dotted around the city, but the one we always return to because of the quality of the coffee is Onna Café. If you're feeling extra decadent, the almond croissant is unbelievably tasty.

(Carrer de Santa Teresa, 1, 08012 Barcelona; www.onnacoffee.com)

69. Visit an Architectural Park Designed by Gaudi

Gaudi is, of course, one of the most beloved architects in Spain, and indeed the world. While in Barcelona, we advise looking beyond the Sagrada Familia and checking out some of his other more obscure works. Park Guell is a park with landscaping and architectural features that was created by Gaudi over the course of about 15 years, and it contains his trademark organic, swirling shapes. Inside, you can also find a house where the architect lived, and it's now the Gaudi House Museum.

(www.parkguell.cat)

70. Do Some Hipster Shopping on Carrer Riera Baixa

Something that you are bound to notice as you walk the streets of Barcelona is that the local people are truly very cool. And if you would like a slice of that uber-cool for yourself, you have to shop where the local hipsters shop, and in Barcelona that always means a place called Carrer Riera Baixa. This is a complex with second hand stores, record shops, tattoo parlours, and everything else that your hipster needs could possibly desire.

(Carrer de la Riera Baixa, 08001 Barcelona)

71. Take in a Classic Modernist Building, the Barcelona Pavilion

One of the most unique buildings in Barcelona is the Barcelona Pavilion, which diverts from most styles used in the city, and instead has a clean, modern feel. It was created in 1929 for the International Exposition and makes use of materials such as marble, red onyx, and travertine. The clean lines of the building create spatial illusions with the reflected light, and it's a wonderful place to visit to take in some peace and elegant design.

72. Enjoy a Mix of Spanish-Argentinian Food at Bitacora

One of the best things about being in Barcelona is trying all of the yummy Catalan food, but if you fancy something a little bit different, then head to Bitacora, a restaurant that mixes the very best of Spanish and Argentinian cuisine. If you want a fantastic steak, this is the place to come to, and there is also a terrace to really make the evening special.

(C/ Balboa, 1, 08003 Barcelona)

73. Lose Yourself in the Horta Labyrinth

Created all the way back in 1791, the Horta Labyrinth is the oldest garden to be found in Barcelona, and we'd say the grandest as well, giving a unique insight into the extravagances of the Spanish monarchy in Catalonia. The central element of the park is a labyrinth formation comprising two metre high hedges that link together to form a maze. Visiting this park is a charming way to enjoy history and the outdoors with kids.

(Passeig dels Castanyers, 1, 08035 Barcelona; http://guia.barcelona.cat/detall/parc-del-laberint-d-horta_92086011952.html)

74. Party With Locals at the Cruilla Barcelona Festival

Barcelona has an incredible summer festival scene, and while you might have heard about Sonar and Primavera Sound before, you might not have heard about Cruilla Barcelona Festival. This is definitely more of a local festival, but is actually the city's top summer festival, showcasing around 40 concerts across 3 days. It takes places in July each year, and has previously attracted incredible talent such as The Prodigy, Pet Shop Boys, and The Lumineers.

(www.cruillabarcelona.com/en/cruilla-festival)

75. Stroll Around Poblenou Cemetery

Okay, so we know that walking around a graveyard sounds like a pretty macabre thing to do on holiday, and you might not have it at the top of your Barcelona to-do list, but we actually think that Poblenou is very beautiful in its own creepy way and is worth visiting if you have a couple of hours to spare. Forget drab grey tombstones, here you're more likely to find incredibly ornate Neoclassical and Neogothic tombs and mausoleums that date back to the 18th century.

(Av. Icària, s/n, 08005 Barcelona)

76. Shop for Local Treats at Fira Artesana

Fira Artesana is a market that only takes place on the first Friday and Saturday of each month, but it's well worth etching it into your diary if you are interested in food products made locally. This market is best known for selling exquisite local honey, as well as things like homemade cakes and honey infused cheeses. Almost everything on display makes for a perfect and slightly unusual gift.

(Plaça del Pi, 08002 Barcelona)

77. Be Wowed by the Catedral de la Seu

Catedral de la Seu is otherwise known as Barcelona Cathedral and is widely considered as the most important church in the city. This church is the seat of the Archbishop of Barcelona, and so it's still a place where you can see services today, but it does have a long history. The church was constructed between the 13th and the 15th centuries, and is mostly in the Gothic style. This is supposed to be one of the darkest cathedrals in the world, with shadows enveloping the whole structure.

(Placita de la Seu, s/n, 08002 Barcelona; www.catedralbcn.org)

78. Celebrate a Local Festival Called Sant Joan

Something unique about Catalonia is that there is a huge emphasis placed on the Summer Solstice, the shortest night of the year, which always takes place towards the end of June. The celebrations in Barcelona are truly magnificent, and it all culminates in the Feast of Sant Joan. As well as a slap up meal, you will be able to experience bonfires and fireworks through the city, with the fires representing the fertility and wealth of the sun.

79. Watch a Movie at Cinema Malda

There are plenty of things to see and do for every kind of tourist visiting Barcelona, but there are times when everybody needs a quiet night watching a great movie. When that moment strikes, be sure to head to the Cinema Malda, which is no ordinary movie theatre. This well loved cinema shows arthouse and indie movies so that your night at the cinema still feels like a special treat.

(Carrer del Pi, 5, 08002 Barcelona; www.cinemamalda.com)

80. Tuck Into Incredible Botifarra at Pork Boig Per Tu

If you haven't tucked into botifarra then you really haven't experienced Catalan cuisine as this is one of the most delicious and respected dishes to emerge from Catalonia, and you can find it in many restaurants in Barcelona. But what exactly is it? Botifarra is a sausage that contains no fat and does not need to be cooked. Pork Boig Per Tu serves up the best botifarra in the city, so do check it out.

(Carrer del Consolat de Mar, 15, 08003 Barcelona; http://porkboigpertu.com)

81. Find Inner Peace at Casa Virupa

Barcelona is a vibrant place and it can be noisy. That's great if you are looking for shows and parties and music, but if you are taken by the simpler things in life, you might be interested in a place that goes by the name of Casa Viripa. This house is located on a hill just outside of the city, and was created in the Buddhist tradition. Whether you would like to try mindfulness meditation for the first time, or you are interested in a longer retreat, this place will have something for you.

(c/ castell s/n, 08511 Tavertet, Barcelona; www.casavirupa.com)

82. Dance Dance Dance at the Annual Circuit Festival

If you are a gay traveller with plans to visit Barcelona, you absolutely need to know about the yearly Circuit Festival, which is hosted every August. This is one seriously epic party that attracts around 70,000 visitors each year. You can expect pool parties, DJs playing all night long on the beach, and masses of gay people having a really great time in Barcelona. Will you be there?

(https://circuitfestival.net/barcelona)

83. Get Decadent at the Churreria Laietana

If you have something of a sweet tooth, you will no doubt want to chow down on plenty of churros while you are in the country. If you have not had a churro before they are essentially long cylinders of batter that are covered in cinnamon sugar, and then typically dipped into melted chocolate or a cup of drinking chocolate. At Churreria Laietana in Barcelona you can eat the churros hot from the fryer, and they are very reasonably priced.

(Via Laietana, 46, 08003 Barcelona)

84. Take in the View From the Columbus Monument

Barcelona is a very attractive city indeed, but you can only appreciate how beautiful it is from the ground up with a very limited perspective. To take in all of its glory, you need to ascend to somewhere with a view, and the Columbus Monument is the perfect place for exactly that. The column and statue of Columbus is placed where he arrived in Barcelona in 1493 after discovering the New World. There is a platform you can ascend that has an outstanding view.

(Plaça Portal de la pau, 08001 Barcelona)

85. Say Hi to the Animals at Barcelona Zoo

When you're travelling with kids and want to keep them entertained for a little while, a trip to the zoo is never going to be a bad idea. There are all kinds of animals at Barcelona Zoo, so whether you are into creepy crawlies or huge gorillas, there will be something to fascinate you. Little kids will be very enamoured by the petting zoo, where they can food animals, and by the train that takes visitors on a journey throughout the outdoor space.

(Parc de la Ciutadella, 08003 Barcelona; www.zoobarcelona.cat)

86. Learn About the Design World at Design Museum of Barcelona

If you're an arts and design lover through and through, make sure that you don't miss the Design Museum of Barcelona, a cutting edge place for design and fashion that is one of the lesser known museums in the city. There's more than 70,000 objects in the museum that draw a line between the city's history and present through design objects such as jewellery, textiles, glassware, graphic design, and more.

(Plaça de les Glòries Catalanes, 37, 08018 Barcelona; http://ajuntament.barcelona.cat/museudeldisseny/)

87. Watch an Alternative Show at Sala Hiroshima

Barcelona is a very dynamic and artsy city, so there is really something in the local arts scene for everyone to enjoy. If you would prefer to see something contemporary instead of a flamenco show or a ballet performance, then you might like the kind of performances that are staged at a theatre called Sala Hiroshima. You can expect alternative performances, as well as a rather lovely on-site bar.

(Carrer de Vila i Vilà, 67, 08004 Barcelona;

http://www.hiroshima.cat/?lang=en)

88. Eat the Best Paella of Your Life at Can Sole

A trip to Spain would not really be a trip to Spain without tucking into a hearty plateful of Paella. Ok, so paella, the most famous of Spanish dishes, is actually not from Barcelona but from Valencia, but this doesn't mean that you can't find plenty of incredible paella goodness around the streets of the city. Our paella pick goes to a restaurant by the name of Can Sole. Their paella is jam packed with fresh seafood, and the portions are beyond generous.

(Carrer de Sant Carles, 4, 08003 Barcelona;
http://restaurantcansole.com)

89. Get to Grips With Local History at Barcelona City History Museum

Barcelona is a place where the sun shines throughout the year, and where the cocktails are always flowing, but it's also a fascinating city with a lot of incredible history, and you can learn loads more about it at the Barcelona City History Museum. This museum will take you on a journey way back to the Roman times, and you'll even be able to see Roman excavations up close. The audio guide is included in the entrance fee and will give you a comprehensive understanding of the city.

(Plaça del Rei, s/n, 08002 Barcelona; www.museuhistoria.bcn.es)

90. Take a Hike Through Montjuic

While it does have some great beaches and a couple of parks, this is really a city for urban dwellers rather than nature lovers. But if you do fancy breathing in some fresh air, strapping on your hiking boots, and going for a hike, Montjuic hill, which overlooks the city from the southwest is a great place to get your walk on. This hill is no Kilimanjaro so if you have moderate fitness, it should be fine, and the reward of visiting Montjuic Castle at the end makes it totally worth it.

91. Take in a Football Match at Camp Nou

If you are a sports fan, it's pretty much needless to say that you need to take in a football match while you're in Barcelona because football is a sporting obsession of the city, and indeed the nation. The local football club plays at an impressive stadium called Camp Nou, which with a seating capacity of around 99,000 people is actually the largest football stadium in all of Europe. When a goal is scored and the crowd roars, the atmosphere is electric. *(C. d'Aristides Maillol, 12, 08028 Barcelona; www.fcbarcelona.com/club/facilities/new-camp-nou)*

92. Eat in Picasso's Favourite Café

Barcelona has a thriving café culture, and there's no shortage of places where you can stop for a strong cup of coffee and a pastry, but there is no café that's quite like Els 4 Gats. This café opened in the latter half of the 19th century, and it quickly became a hangout and meeting place for Catalonia's Modernist artists like Pablo Picasso and Ramon Casas I Carbo. The poster that stands on the corner of the street outside of the café was designed by Picasso himself.

(Carrer de Montsió, 3, 08002 Barcelona; www.4gats.com)

93. Enjoy an Old Fashioned Street Party, Festa de Sant Roc

The locals in Barcelona sure do know how to take to the streets and party, and this is never more evident than during the Festa de Sant Roc, the city's largest street party, which is hosed in the Gothic Quarter during mid-August each year. This epic street party actually lasts for five days, and contains something for everyone. You can expect parades, concerts, workshops, kids activities, and loads more besides.

94. Discover a World of Egyptian Artefacts at Museu Egipci

The Museu Egipci, or Egyptian Museum of Barcelona, is the only museum in all of Spain that is dedicated to

Ancient Egypt, and it's a great place for history buffs to pass an afternoon. Inside you will find a stunning 1200 examples of Ancient Egyptian art and artefacts, which each shed their own light on the culture of the Pharaohs.

(Calle Valencia, 284, 08007 Barcelona; www.museuegipci.com)

95. Discover Local Craft Beers at Edge Brewing

Considering that Spain is a beer loving nation to say the least, it might be a little surprising that there aren't a tonne of well known Spanish beer brands. But who needs famous brands when a place like Barcelona has some stunning craft beers anyway? If you're a beer lover, then be sure to make time for a trip to Edge Brewing, a place founded by two Americans to bring craft beers to Barcelona. Book the brewery tour if you really want the inside track.

(Carrer de Llull, 62, 08005 Barcelona; http://edgebrewing.com)

96. Feel the Buzz of Creativity at Palo Alto Market

To get to know a city, we love to stroll its markets, and while Palo Alto Market is certainly a new kid on the block of Barcelona's market scene, we really feel that it captures the essence of the city perfectly. This is an outdoor market that brings together fashion, food, art, and music together in the coolest ways. You can pick up some exquisitely designed pieces at very reasonable prices, and all while listening to awesome live music and tucking into delicious street food. Just open on weekends.

(Carrer dels Pellaires, 30, 08019 Barcelona;
https://paloaltomarket.com/en)

97. Have the Best Ice Cream of Your Life at Gelaaati di Marco

The temperatures in Barcelona can really soar, and our favourite way to cool down from the heat is with a big scoop of ice cream (or three). Of course, there's no shortage of places where you can indulge with ice cream, but we think the best place of the bunch is an ice cream joint called Gelaaati di Marco. Our favourite flavours are cheesecake and fig, but truly everything tastes exceptional.

(Carrer de la Llibreteria, 7, 08002 Barcelona;
www.gelaaati.com/en)

98. Enjoy a World of Croquettes From Reina Croqueta

Croquettes are one of the most quintessentially Spanish foods, and this means that you have to tuck into a plateful at least once during your time in Barcelona. For us, nothing beats the croquettes of Reina Croqueta, because what else would you expect from a food truck that is named after the dish? You can have them filled with deliciousness like Roquefort cheese, salt cod, and many other options.

(www.reinacroqueta.com)

99. Shop Til Your Drop at Mercantic

If you're struggling for something to do on a Sunday morning when all of the museums are closed, by not head to a local antiques market called Mercantic? A series of timber huts are filled with things like antique art pieces, vintage furniture, bric-a-brac, and more. There's also plenty of food and drink on offer so you won't go hungry, and sometimes there is even live music playing in the outdoors.

(Av. de Rius i Taulet, 120, 08173 Sant Cugat del Vallès, Barcelona; www.mercantic.com)

100. Have an Artsy Day at the Barcelona Museum of Contemporary Art

Barcelona is a pretty sunny city, but if you happen to be there of a cloudy day, there are still plenty of things to do, because this is one of the museum and gallery capitals of Europe. If you'd like to see something cutting edge, we would recommend the Barcelona Museum of Contemporary Art. Although it's just a few blocks from the Gothic centre of the city, the design of this building is totally different: sleek and modern. There is a focus on Catalan and Spanish art from 1945 onwards.

(Plaça dels Àngels, 1, 08001 Barcelona; www.macba.cat)

101. Drink With Locals at El Paraigua

There's no denying that the local people of Barcelona do like a drink or two, and actually the city can seem even more lively at night than it does during the day. One of our favourite bars to visit on any night of the week is El Paraigua (which translates into The Umbrella), and it doesn't seem like much from the outside. Head downstairs and you will find plush sofas, ample space for a dance, and very strong cocktails indeed.

(Carrer del Pas de l'Ensenyança, 2, 08002 Barcelona; www.elparaigua.com)

Before You Go...

Thanks for reading **101 Amazing Things to Do in Barcelona.** We hope that it makes your trip a memorable one!

Have a great trip, and don't eat too much tapas!

Team 101 Amazing Things

Printed in Great Britain
by Amazon